Michael Jackson

ABDO
Publishing Company

Big Buddy BOOKS
Buddy Bios

by **Sarah Tieck**

VISIT US AT
www.abdopublishing.com

Published by ABDO Publishing Company, 8000 West 78th Street, Edina, Minnesota 55439.

Copyright © 2011 by Abdo Consulting Group, Inc. International copyrights reserved in all countries. No part of this book may be reproduced in any form without written permission from the publisher. Big Buddy Books™ is a trademark and logo of ABDO Publishing Company.

Printed in the United States of America, North Mankato, Minnesota.
102010
012011

♻ PRINTED ON RECYCLED PAPER

Coordinating Series Editor: Rochelle Baltzer
Contributing Editors: Megan M. Gunderson, BreAnn Rumsch, Marcia Zappa
Graphic Design: Maria Hosley
Cover Photograph: *AP Photo*: Cliff Schiappa.
Interior Photographs/Illustrations: *AP Photo*: AP Photo (pp. 9, 15), Diane Bondareff/PictureGroup via AP IMAGES (p. 16), Mark Davis/Hope for Haiti Now (p. 29), Imaginechina via AP Images (p. 25), Jens Meyer (p. 25), James Mitchell/Ebony Collection via AP Images (pp. 7, 29), Leroy Patton/Ebony Collection via AP Images (p. 11), Reed Saxon, file (p. 17), Matt Sayles (pp. 28, 29), Wally Skalij, Pool, file (p. 27), Isaac Sutton/Ebony Collection via AP Images (p. 13); *Getty Images*: Blank Archives (p. 21), Phil Dent/Redferns (p. 19), Kevork Djansezian (p. 26), Kevin Mazur/WireImage (p. 5), Al Messerschmidt (p. 23).

Library of Congress Cataloging-in-Publication Data

Tieck, Sarah, 1976-
  Michael Jackson : music legend / Sarah Tieck.
    p. cm. -- (Big buddy biographies)
  ISBN 978-1-61714-703-6
  1. Jackson, Michael, 1958-2009--Juvenile literature. 2. Rock musicians--United States--Biography--Juvenile literature. I. Title.
  ML3930.J25T54 2011
  782.42166092--dc22
  [B]
                                        2010037087

Michael Jackson

Contents

Music Legend

   Michael Jackson was a famous singer, songwriter, and dancer. He was best known for singing popular music. Even though he died in 2009, his music lives on.
   Michael's ideas and style changed music. He sold millions of records. And, he is in the Rock and Roll Hall of Fame!

Wisconsin

LAKE MICHIGAN

Michigan

Gary

Illinois

Missouri

Indiana

Ohio

N
W E
S

Kentucky

Family Ties

Michael Joseph Jackson was born in Gary, Indiana, on August 29, 1958. Michael's parents are Joseph and Katherine Jackson.

Michael came from a very big family! His older sisters are Rebbie and La Toya. His older brothers are Jackie, Tito, Jermaine, and Marlon. Michael's younger brother is Randy. His younger sister is Janet.

Did you know...

Michael was close to his sister Janet. Today, Janet is a famous singer and dancer, too!

The Jackson family lived in a small house in Gary, Indiana. Even though they moved, people still think of it as their house. Over the years, Rebbie (*left*), Katherine (*right*), and other family members have visited it.

Starting Out

The Jackson kids showed talent for music. Around 1963, Michael and his older brothers formed a music group called the Jackson 5.
People noticed that Michael was a strong singer. This was surprising because he was so young! Soon, Michael became the group's lead singer.

Big Break

The Jackson 5 sang **rhythm and blues** music. They became popular near Gary. Soon, they were traveling around the United States to **perform**.

Around 1968, famous record **producer** Berry Gordy Jr. heard about their talent. He wanted to work with the Jackson 5 to record their music.

Did you know...

The Jackson 5 sang at the well-known Apollo Theater. It is in an area of New York City called Harlem. Many famous African-American singers have performed there.

Famous singer Diana Ross had also heard the Jackson 5. She wanted to help them **release** a record. In 1969, they released their first album with Motown Records. It was called *Diana Ross Presents the Jackson 5*.

The album had many hit songs. The first hit was "I Want You Back." Others were "ABC" and "I'll Be There." People still like these songs today!

In 1976, the Jackson 5 became the Jacksons. Michael's brother Randy replaced Jermaine in the group. The Jacksons even had their own television show. Michael's sisters often appeared on it, too.

Changing Directions

The Jacksons continued to be successful until about 1984. But in 1971, Michael also began a solo **career**. He had his own hit songs. But, many people still thought of him as "Little Michael." So, Michael worked to show them he was grown up.

Michael started working with famous **producer** Quincy Jones on a new album. In 1979, Michael **released** *Off the Wall*. It became a hit! People liked Michael's changing style.

Quincy Jones (*right*) is a well-known producer. In 1984, he won a Grammy for his work with Michael. Grammy Awards recognize excellence in music.

Superstar

In 1982, Michael _____ an album called *Thriller*. Seven of its nine songs became top-ten hits! These included "Thriller," "Billie Jean," and "Beat It." People were excited by Michael's style of singing.

Thriller was Michael's most successful album. It became the best-selling album of all time!

Michael was famous for wearing a sparkly glove on one hand.

Did you know...

Michael made a music video for "Thriller" that was 14 minutes long! It featured Michael dancing with monsters. People loved it!

Throughout his solo career, Michael won 13 Grammy Awards for his work. He won eight for *Thriller* alone (*left*)!

Moonwalk

Michael's music is known for its dance beat. People say he was a very skilled dancer. When he did a dance move, it often became popular!

While **performing** "Billie Jean" in 1983, Michael did a dance move he called the moonwalk. Fans became very excited about the moonwalk. Soon, people around the world were learning it!

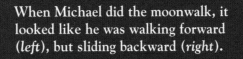

When Michael did the moonwalk, it looked like he was walking forward (*left*), but sliding backward (*right*).

Helping Hands

Michael enjoyed helping others. In 1985, he and singer Lionel Richie wrote a song called "We Are the World." Many famous singers recorded the song together. Money from record sales helped people in Africa.

After this, Michael continued to help people. He often gave money for causes he cared about. And, he used his fame to get others to help, too.

Hit after Hit

In 1987, Michael **released** an album called *Bad*. In 1991, he put out *Dangerous*. Both albums had several hit songs.

In 1995, Michael released *HIStory: Past, Present and Future, Book 1*. Then, Michael went on a world tour. More than 4 million fans saw him **perform**!

Michael was known for doing large, exciting shows. One famous show was at the 1993 Super Bowl. Some people tuned in just to see Michael!

Fans around the world were excited to see the movie *This Is It*. They got to watch Michael perform old hit songs and a new one.

Later Years

In the 1990s and early 2000s, Michael faced some personal challenges. He had less success with his music. Then in 2009, he planned to do 50 concerts in London, England. It was called the This Is It tour.

Michael died unexpectedly on June 25, 2009. People all over the world were sad. That fall, a movie called *This Is It* was **released**. It shows Michael practicing for the 2009 concerts. An album called *This Is It* also came out.

Michael sold about 750 million albums during his career.

Off the Stage

Michael had three children. His sons are Prince Michael and Prince Michael II. His daughter is Paris. When Michael was not working, he spent time with his children. They traveled all over the world together. Michael was also close to his mother, his brothers, and his sisters.

Paris spoke to thousands of people at her father's memorial. She told them he was a good dad.

Did you know...

Prince Michael II is also called "Blanket."

Buzz

Michael was very famous. During his **career**, he met U.S. presidents and other important people. He was often in newspapers and magazines.

Throughout Michael's life, his work stayed popular. Michael's music and style gave other singers ideas. And, Michael won many awards for his music. Even though Michael Jackson is gone, his work remains important!

Singers such as Usher (*above*), Beyoncé (*left*), and Justin Timberlake (*below*) look to Michael's work for ideas.

Snapshot

★**Name**: Michael Joseph Jackson

★**Birthday**: August 29, 1958

★**Birthplace**: Gary, Indiana

★**Albums**: *Diana Ross Presents the Jackson 5, Off the Wall, Thriller, Bad, Dangerous, HIStory: Past, Present and Future, Book 1, This Is It*

★**Date of Death**: June 25, 2009

Important Words

career work a person does to earn money for living.

perform to do something that requires skill in front of an audience.

producer a person who oversees the making of a movie, a play, an album, or a radio or television show.

release to make available to the public.

rhythm (RIH-thuhm) **and blues** a form of popular music that features a strong beat. It is inspired by jazz, gospel, and blues styles.

Web Sites

To learn more about Michael Jackson, visit ABDO Publishing Company online. Web sites about Michael Jackson are featured on our Book Links page. These links are routinely monitored and updated to provide the most current information available.

www.abdopublishing.com

Index